Pocket
Guide to
Facilitating
Human
Connections

Rod Lee + Chad Littlefield

D1593932

Pocket Guide to Facilitating Human Connections

Copyright © 2017 Chad Littlefield and Rod Lee

All rights reserved. No part of this book may be reproduced or retransmitted without the written permission of the publisher.

Photos by Paul Girgis

Printed in the USA by Minibük

For author booking information:

chad@weand.me

rod@upstagecommunications.com

ISBN 978-0-9964239-7-7

Human connection is being filtered more than ever. This is precisely the reason we need to be disciplined in creating connections that remain human.

Table of Contents

Key Concepts

Connection Activities

Communication & Cooperation Activities

Trust Activities

We! Connect Cards™ Activities

Introduction

Chad and I have a passion for our field. We have used that passion and this mini book format to distill our craft into a usable tool, drawing on our combined 30 years of experience in the field of experiential learning to acknowledge its history while also looking to the future. In today's hyperconnected world, technology has become increasingly integral to work; and as such, the human connection is being filtered more than ever. This is precisely the reason we need to be disciplined in creating connections that remain human. Facilitating the types of activities found in this book is intended to do just that.

This book is the result of countless conversations and interactions over the course of two years. It is a small book with large implications. I met Chad Littlefield when he was a student, and he made an immediate impact. I knew we would work together beyond our time as faculty and graduate student. Well, here we are, having co-created our first publication, formatted to provide exceptional value for its size. It's said that "good things come in small packages"; we trust you will find that true of this publication.

It was clear from the outset that Chad and I wanted something "different" as our first published work – not just something that provides great information for those who want to lead an experiential program, but something that can be a reference, real time. This mini book format provides a resource that fits in your pocket. We also realize the importance of having resources beyond the tools we carry with us, and so we hope you find our references helpful to your work, as well.

Enjoy the journey.

Yours in Adventure,

Rod + Chad

Key
Concepts

pp. 8 - 41

You always have a
choice.

— Erik Tyler —

Challenge by Choice

Challenge by Choice is a philosophy used in experiential and adventure programming. Karl Rohnke, while working for Project Adventure, is credited with having coined this phrase. The principle is very simple at its core but can be complex to manage as we lead activities:

Every participant has the choice to participate at a level of their own choosing.

For every program, our goal is always to empower participants to make choices that will help them learn and then to apply their learnings to other environments outside of the program itself. This may be in the workplace, in their personal life, or in any other situation where they may find themselves interacting with others. Challenge by Choice is the core philosophy in moving towards this goal.

Vulnerability is the birthplace of innovation, creativity, and change.

- Brené Brown -

Comfort Zone Model

Understanding that every individual will have an experience that is specific to themselves is an important realization for a facilitator. We can appreciate this concept through understanding the Comfort Zone Model. The model has been widely used in Adventure / Experiential Education and has roots in both Piaget's cognitive development work and Vygotsky's Zones of Proximal Development.

We all know what it is like to feel comfortable. While it is possible to learn in this **Comfort Zone**, stepping outside of our comfort zone and into the **Learning Zone** heightens our senses and allows for more learning to occur. We must be careful as leaders and facilitators to offer experiences that encourage our participants to choose to move into their Learning Zone. The **Panic Zone**, however, should be avoided, since it stifles learning and can even create potential for psychological harm. As leaders and facilitators, we need to be observant and, wherever signs of panic begin to surface among participants, to offer choices that enable them to move between their Comfort Zone and Learning Zone.

COMFORT ZONE

Safe • Secure • Stable • Easy • Bored • Comfortable • Predictable • Normal

LEARNING ZONE

Willing to risk • Anticipating • Exhiliarated • Challenged • Alive • Excited • Discovering

PANIC ZONE

Stressed • Fearful • Tense • Exhausted • Fed Up • Worried • Anxious • Annoyed • Frusterated • Tired

Planning is bringing the future into the present so that you can do something about it now.

– Alan Lakein –

Sequencing

As leaders and facilitators, providing an appropriate sequence of activities for a group is as important as the activities themselves. The specific sequence will depend on the actual group you are working with, the goals of the program and the time frame you have.

It is always best to start any program with some sort of **Connection** activity. This provides the group with an opportunity to get immersed into the methodology of experiential learning, while also helping to reduce any anxiety within the group. Focus on one-to-one or small-group interactions that give people the opportunity to share their names and learn a little about each other. Often, a series of different Connection activities is needed; 10 to 30 minutes of this basic relationship building is essential. Connection before content broadens the possibilities for the rest of a program.

Once the group has developed a level of comfort with one another, it's time to move on to **Communication & Cooperation** exercises, which bring the group to a greater understanding of how they can work together effectively. Finally, **Trust** exercises build on the foundation of continued team success. A group or team where trust is lacking cannot function at a high level. (With longer programs, we personally tend to intersperse trust exercises within a sequence of communication and cooperation exercises.)

NOTE: If you want to set a group up for failure, start with a trust exercise! That may put some of your participants in the **Panic Zone** right out of the gate. Trust takes time to build but can be created through a good sequence of relationship building and opportunities to work together.

All life is an
experiment.

- Ralph Waldo Emerson -

Experiential Learning Cycle

The Experiential Learning Cycle (ELC), based on the work by Kolb (1984), is shown below. When used skillfully, the ELC framework allows a team to learn from concrete experiences and to extend these learnings into a real-world context. As a leader and facilitator, you will guide the group through all four stages as part of a program. We also utilize this model to help us debrief (more on that later).

Everyone and
everything around
you is your teacher.

- Ken Keyes Jr. -

Experiential Training and Development

Experiential Training and Development (ETD) is an approach to organizational learning which is used to develop relationships, enhance performance, or influence organization-wide improvements. Applicable for individuals or groups of adult learners, ETD trainings and consultations typically include *action*, *reflection*, *discussion*, *transfer*, and *support*.

Research shows that ETD is one of the most effective tools for facilitating organizational and personal transformation. The best ETD consists of time-tested methods blended with cutting-edge content. It focuses on specific outcomes and is led by experienced practitioners who will be well equipped to help your organization, your leaders, or your people make tangible and meaningful transfers between a learning experience and ongoing organizational challenges.

This model breaks down Experiential Training and Development into the depth of impact, focus, and duration of each type of service offered.

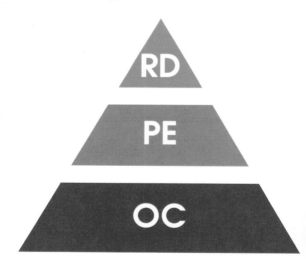

Thanks to the ETD Alliance for letting us share this content.

www.etdalliance.com

RELATIONSHIP DEVELOPMENT

▶ Activities that build awareness of relationships

▶ Half day to 3 days in length

▶ High energy and fun

PERFORMANCE ENHANCEMENT

▶ Skill building for people, systems, and content

▶ Multiple half-day to single full-day programs

▶ Involves in-depth assessment, pre-work and follow up

ORGANIZATIONAL CONSULTING

▶ Changing how business is done, transforming business culture

▶ Ongoing work to change systems and work on continuous improvement

▶ Custom processes for specific business setting

If you don't
have clarity of
ideas, you're just
communicating
sheer sound.

- Yo-Yo Ma -

Briefing

Clearly introducing an activity is a key part of a facilitator's role. We have developed an acronym to help you remember to cover all components of a good briefing: FOGS. If you use FOGS, you will literally keep your groups "out of the fog" by providing the clarity they need to attempt the challenges you present to them.

This framework can be used to brief or introduce a single activity, a meeting, an entire program, or even an overarching goal of an organization. Reusing the FOGS framework throughout a program can help weave a thread between people's experience and the content.

F **rame It!** = Tell a story; be aware of your audience; use metaphors or connections to the program goals

O **bjective** = Clearly state the overall goal to be accomplished or the purpose of an activity

G **uidelines** = Explain the "rules to play by" or the parameters and constraints within which to operate

S **afety** = Make participants aware of any potential physical and emotional risks

We always finish FOGS by simply asking, "Do you have any questions?" This allows the group members an opportunity to clarify anything that is still "foggy" before they start.

We will use this framework for describing all of our activities throughout the remainder of this Pocket Guide.

The value in an idea
lies in using it.

– Thomas Edison –

Debriefing

Debriefing helps us provide meaning to the experience. We do not have to debrief every activity we facilitate, especially icebreakers and energizers.

Solid debriefing has perhaps the greatest impact on a group.

Our good friend Nate Folan used the Experiential Learning Cycle as a framework for debriefing in his book, The Hundredth Monkey (2012). Thanks, Nate, for giving us permission to share your work within our own. Here's an overview of debriefing.

Nate Folan's three tiers of debriefing
to help structure more productive
reflection of any experience.

Recreational Debrief

▶ A Recreational Debrief invites the group simply to reflect on their experience. There is value in remembering and sharing vivid moments of awesomeness!

▶ We like to offer specific shared language like "Rewind The Tape" to help groups debrief at this level.

Educational Debrief

▶ The next level, the Educational Debrief, appropriately meets program goals that seek more depth and cognitive learning. Participants at this phase are invited or guided to analyze their experience and make meaning that may be abstract in nature. The goal at this level is for participants to build more knowledge and awareness around a particular topic.

▶ We like to use questions such as "What did you learn from that activity?" or "What worked well for you?" to help groups debrief at this level.

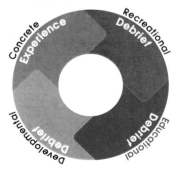

Developmental Debrief

▶ The third and final level, the Developmental Debrief, provides the most depth and moves the debrief beyond word. This level of debrief should prepare participants for action by focusing on "What are we going to do with what we learned?" A simple way to look at this is to acknowledge and appreciate the learning and then go play with it!

▶ We like to use questions such as "How can you apply what you have learned to the next activity (or your life outside of this program)?" or "What is one behavior you will change when you get back to work?"

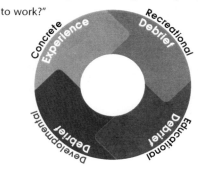

Nate's adaptation of Kolb's Experiential Learning Cycle provides a simple guide for debriefing. We can choose what level we would like to debrief at, based on our experience with the group and the goals of the program.

There are also many other books and debriefing tools that can help with this process. See our resources section for more information on these.

Debriefing with Quotes

Throughout this book you will find numerous quotes that we have researched to create a connection to the content. Quotes are a very efficient way of creating an emotional connection through the words of another.

Quotes can also be used in the debrief to connect to the key learnings that have materialized as part of the activity. We have found that using a well-known quote followed by inviting actual quotes from participants during an activity is a very rich way of connecting people both to the experience and the learnings that emerge. A good quote can also be used as part of an activity brief to "Frame It!" and to infuse meaning into an experience.

The most powerful quotes in an experiential program can come from within the group. As a leader and facilitator, take the time to listen for these hidden perspectives. We hope you enjoy the quotes we share with you and we hope you go out to discover many more.

More quotes can be found at **www.weand.me/quotes**

The biggest risk is not taking any risk. In a world that is changing really quickly, the only strategy that is guaranteed to fail is not taking risks.

– Mark Zuckerberg –

Risk Management

As we facilitate a group, we need to be able to manage the risk on two levels: possible physical risks and emotional risks. If we use our FOGS framework for briefing an activity, we can highlight possible risks and manage them.

At the core, our role is to provide a safe environment within which the individuals within the group can make choices. These choices provide the opportunity for learning and ultimately behavioral change.

Physical Risk

▶ Here, we can highlight the simple concept of taking care of each other physically. The basic premise is that there is nothing worth getting hurt for in any program. Participants sometimes need to be reminded of physical risk as an activity progresses, especially when engagement levels are high and the group wants to complete a particular challenge.

▶ In our briefing, we can highlight things like being aware of others as we move, moving at an appropriate pace, helping each other with balance, etc.

▶ We choose to use words to encourage the correct behaviors rather than focusing on negative behaviors.

Emotional Risk

▶ Emotional risk is harder to manage, since each individual will have a subjective and uniquely personal experience. We need to be aware of those behaviors that might indicate that a participant may be close to the Panic Zone.

▶ As leaders and facilitators, we need to be hyper vigilant of the affect of each group member and try to offer many possible choices as to how they might choose to participate. For example, if a person does not want to participate in a particular challenge, we often offer this person a choice to become an observer. They will report what they observed as part of the debrief. This keeps them engaged throughout the activity until they are ready to participate again.

Index of
Activities

Connection
Activities

Communication
& Cooperation
Activities

Trust Activities

We! Connect
Cards Activities

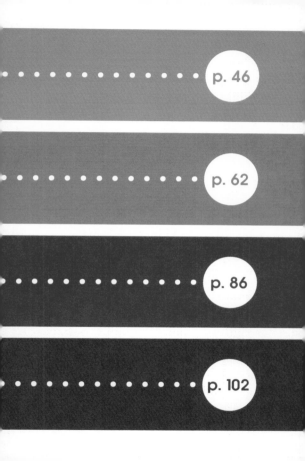

Connection
Activities

Connection activities are designed to invite a group to get to know one another better and to form the foundations of relationships. Each activity provides a highly interactive, non-threatening experience for people to learn about each other while having fun. Often, there is no need to debrief connection activities. We intentionally created each activity write up to be brief in order to allow space for your own interpretation. Be creative in your facilitation! Mold each activity to best suit your group and your environment. Activities in this category include:

▶ Who?
▶ What's in a Name?
▶ Incorporations
▶ Handshakes
▶ Ubuntu Cards - Fast Find
▶ Ubuntu Cards - Olympics

The meeting of
two personalities
is like the contact
of two chemical
substances;
if there is any
reaction, both are
transformed.

- Carl Jung -

We must establish a personal connection with each other. Connection before content. Without relatedness, no work can occur.

– Peter Block –

Frame It!

"Have you ever forgotten somebody's name? Then this activity is for you."

Objective

Learn names without having to know anybody

Guidelines

✓ Form a circle with a volunteer standing in the middle

✓ The volunteer randomly points at a person and calls out "Who?" as that person walks toward them

✓ The chosen participant will say their name and switch places with the first volunteer in the center

✓ The new participant will continue the game by pointing to someone else

✓ Continue until everyone has been called into the circle

Connection

What's in a
Name?

Frame It!

"Welcome to the Name Olympics. You all have a chance to go for the gold."

Objective

Have some fun exploring how the letters in your name compare with the letters in others' names

Guidelines

✓ Tally up the number of letters in your first name, and get into a line from lowest to highest (e.g., Rod (3) or Roderick (8))

✓ Go down the line stating names and the number of letters in each

✓ Additional rounds should be added for first-plus-middle name totals and first-middle-last name totals

Incorporations

Frame It!

"Without knowing it, we each share hundreds of invisible commonalities with one another."

Objective

Find all of "your people" based on a given category

Guidelines

- ✓ Form distinct groups based on the category chosen by facilitator (e.g., favorite season, color of shirt, favorite outdoor activity, etc.)
- ✓ Shout your category in unison and with pride when facilitator points to your group
- ✓ Play multiple rounds and feel free to invite conversation within the groups that form

Handshakes

Frame It!

"When you meet somebody, what are the first things you do?"

Objective

Connect and learn some new handshakes along the way

Guidelines

✓ Introduce a new handshake (e.g., high-five, ankle shake, lumberjack, etc.)
✓ Find a single partner with whom to exchange this handshake and discuss a given question
✓ Repeat this process 3 - 4 times making sure to go back and greet each of your old partners with previously shared handshakes before finding a new partner

UBUNTU

Fast Find

You can find Ubuntu Cards from High 5 Adventure Learning

Frame It!

"Each of us is connected by a common bond. Let's find the common ground that brings us together."

Objective

Find your common objects and swap cards with as many people as possible

Guidelines

✓ Pair up and hold out your card with the large image side facing up

✓ Flip cards to show small image side.

✓ Be the first to call out the image that is common on both your cards and you "win"

✓ Then, immediately swap cards, give your partner a high-five and move on to somebody else

✓ Repeat until the facilitator ends the activity while energy is still high

Connection

UBUNTU

Olympics

You can find Ubuntu Cards from High 5 Adventure Learning

Frame It!

"Each of you has the opportunity to be named the champion in this activity."

Objective

Skillfully navigate your way to the final round of Ubuntu Olympics and cheer on others in the process

Guidelines

✓ Pair up and hold out your card with the small image side facing up
✓ Much like Rock-Paper-Scissor Olympics, be the first to call out the image and you earn the support of your competitor (and their supporters)
✓ "Losers" must cheer on their competitor
✓ Play 1 - 3 rounds until there is an ultimate champion named

Communication
& Cooperation
Activities

Communication & Cooperation activities are designed to invite a group to explore what it means to work effectively together. Through concrete experience and reflection, these activities can bring real-world concepts to life. Each activity provides a level of challenge that will require a team to work together to overcome it. We intentionally created each activity write up to be brief in order to allow space for your own interpretation. Be creative in your facilitation! Mold each activity to best suit your group and your environment. After each activity description, there are tips and sample debrief questions to spark powerful conversations aimed at developing learnings that can be applied outside the context of the activity. Activities in this category include:

▶ Group Juggle
▶ Keypunch
▶ Paper Towers
▶ We! Discover Cards - Travel the World
▶ Zin Monument

Communication
- the human
connection - is the
key to personal and
career success.

- Paul J. Meyer -

The single
biggest problem
in communication
is the illusion that it
has taken place.

- George Bernard Shaw -

Group
Juggle

Objects in play are part of the Body Part Debrief from Training Wheels

Frame It!

"Can anybody juggle? Can anybody group juggle?"

Objective

Create a pattern by tossing an object (or objects) to everyone in the group

Guidelines

✓ Everyone must touch the object once and only once

✓ Object will always start and end with facilitator

✓ Only one object is allowed in your hands at any time

✓ Say the name of the person you are throwing to

✓ If object is dropped, either continue or restart the round

✓ Challenge the group with "warp speed" rounds to improve on time, and/or add more objects to the juggle

Keep this activity light and fun. Don't make a big deal over dropping a ball. Encourage participants to pick up and carry on. This activity is a great conversation starter for how we have many responsibilities to juggle in our lives. Insights into how we manage "balls being dropped" are good for the group to explore.

Debrief

Recreational:

▶ What did the group do when we went from one object to three objects?

Educational:

▶ What were the keys to your success?

Developmental:

▶ What have we learned from this activity that we can apply to our next team challenge?

Keypunch

Frame It!

"It's lunchtime, hunger is setting in and it is your group's goal to dial in the food as quickly as possible."

Objective

Touch all the numbers within a designated area in numerical order as quickly as possible

Guidelines

✓ The group starts out behind a line
✓ The counter will begin when the first member crossing the line
✓ Each participant has to at least touch one number
✓ Only one participant is allowed in the designated area at a time
✓ Only one number may be touched at a time
✓ The timer will end when all members are back over the line

Communication & Cooperation

✓ Time penalties will be given if not every member touched a number, if numbers are touched out of sequence, and if multiple people are in the designated area at one time
✓ The facilitator can decide the time penalties
✓ Play multiple rounds

Tips

It is great to have the team members manage infractions themselves after they have experienced the challenge for the first round. The facilitator does not need to be the "policeman / policewomen." As they manage their open performance in alignment with the "policies," it provides a great opportunity for a conversation around ethical behavior and holding each other to the highest standards.

Debrief

Recreational:

► What strategies did you use to increase your efficiency?

Educational:

► How did you play to each other's strengths in this activity?

Developmental:

► How can you apply what happened in Keypunch to your next project that involves a deadline?

Paper
Towers

Frame It!

"We are constantly building: relationships, reports, ideas, products, and services. The process of building can be complex."

Objective

Construct the tallest freestanding structure possible

Guidelines

✓ Use only:

 ▶ Single piece of 8.5" x 11" paper

 ▶ Scissors

 ▶ 1 foot of scotch tape

✓ Work in groups of 2 - 3 people maximum

✓ 10 minutes allotted before towers are measured

Tips

This is an activity that needs to be facilitated indoors; otherwise paper will fly everywhere! Competition within groups comes out and leads to an opportunity for a conversation around what resources the groups compete for in their work environments and how they manage that reality.

Communication & Cooperation

Debrief

Recreational:

▶ What was it like to compete against your colleagues?

Educational:

▶ How did you manage the competitive environment while still being respectful to your colleagues in other teams?

Developmental:

▶ How can you manage competing priorities in your work to ensure that your team continues to act in appropriate ways?

Travel the
World

We! Discover Cards can be found at **www.weand.me/store**

Frame It!

"Navigating difficult circumstances with a group is tough!"

Objective

Navigate your entire team through a predetermined route on a world map maze

Guidelines

✓ Each team has its own predetermined path across the world maze

✓ Only one person can step onto the world at a given time

✓ You may progress as far as you can on the correct route taking one step at a time

✓ If you make an incorrect step, you will hear a corresponding signal from one team member designated as "air traffic control"

✓ "Air traffic control" will be the only person who knows the predetermined route

✓ Each group member must attempt a travel route before anyone can re-enter the world maze

✓ *Optional*: no talking allowed while a team member is in the maze

Tips

Inviting the group to lay out the cards on the ground in the correct orientation can engage people more in the setup of the activity. Adding a budget element to this activity by "charging" for steps and missteps can increase the need for effective communication and cooperation.

Debrief

Recreational:

▶ What did the group do to support one another?

Educational:

▶ How do the communication dynamics that came up in this activity compare to dynamics at work?

Developmental:

▶ What is one lesson learned from "traveling the world" that can be immediately applied to your life?

Zin
Monument

Frame It!

"In the ancient city of Atlantis, a great monument was constructed in honor of the goddess Diana. It is known as the Zin Monument.

Objective

Figure out which day of the week the Zin Monument was completed

Guidelines

✓ You may only share information on your cards orally
✓ One full deck is required for a team to solve the problem
✓ You have up to 30 minutes to complete this challenge
✓ *Note*: this activity requires intensive problem solving and may not be appropriate in all settings

Tips

This activity is a wonderful analogy to the reality of working in remote teams. It is a great activity to provide opportunities for conversations about communication strategies, managing different perceptions, and finding a common ground.

The source for this activity came from a book entitled *Improving Work Groups: A Practical Manual for Team Building by Dave Francis and Don Young.*

Debrief

Recreational:

▶ What challenges did you overcome as you worked towards solving the Zin Monument puzzle?

Educational:

▶ How did this activity mirror any of the challenges you face on a daily basis at work?

Developmental:

▶ What did you learn from this activity that you can apply to your work? How can you make that happen?

Trust
Activities

Trust activities are designed to begin the conversation about what it takes to build a relationship of trust with another person. Debriefing these experiences is essential to connect people to real trust issues beyond the activity. We intentionally created each activity write up to be brief to allow space for your own interpretation. Keeping safety in mind, be creative in your facilitation! Mold each activity to best suit your group and your environment. After each activity description, there are tips and sample debrief questions to spark powerful conversations aimed at developing learnings that can be applied outside the context of the activity. Activities in this category include:

▶ Ingredients of Trust
▶ Paired compass walk
▶ Trust Zones

Remove trust, and you compromise love, friendship, trade, and leadership.

- Antonio Damasio -

Trust is like blood pressure. It's silent, vital to good health, and if abused it can be deadly.

– Frank Sonnenberg –

Ingredients
of Trust

You can find these cards at **www.weand.me/store**

Frame It!

"Relationships form on a foundation of trust, yet trust can often be invisible. This activity is about making the invisible visible."

Objective

Choose an image to share that represents one crucial ingredient to building a relationship of trust

Guidelines

√ Start with a 2-3 minute round for people to explore a series of images spread out on a surface nearby

√ Invite everyone to select one photo that represents a single ingredient necessary to build a foundation of trust within a group or relationship

√ Have people share their image, why they chose it, and place the image in the center of the circle

Trust

Tips

Spread the images out on a surface that offers enough space for people to move around to get a look at all of the images. When it comes time for people to share, organize the group in a circle to enable everyone to see the images people have chosen and to hear what they have to say.

Trust

Debrief

Recreational:

▶ What was difficult about choosing a single image?

Educational:

▶ What themes did you notice in what the group had to share?

Developmental:

▶ How can we implement some of these ideas to make them a reality?

Paired Compass Walk

Frame It!

"While animals are often masterful at navigating through darkness, people generally are not. This exercise creates an opportunity for you to test your own sense of direction while trusting a partner."

Objective

Trust your own internal compass to blindly navigate you to a destination over 150 feet away

Guidelines

✓ Each person with his eyes closed must be paired with a guide partner who has his eyes open

✓ Choose a destination at least 150 feet away from the starting point

✓ The challenge is to keep your eyes closed for the entire duration of the walk

✓ The guide will call out "STOP" immediately if their partner is at any risk of bumping into someone or something

Trust

Tips

The walkers need to walk with their "bumpers up": hands out in front, palms up, with arms bent and elbows toward the floor. This will provide an added level of protection against walking into others. This is an activity that requires the facilitator to maintain a keen eye toward risk management. Be ready to intervene if needed.

You can also build up to doing this activity in one large Group Compass Walk as well with you as the facilitator managing safety and tracking the group's path.

Debrief

Recreational:

▶ What were you thinking and feeling when we started this activity?

Educational:

▶ How did you overcome any anxiety felt by you or your partner? How did you coach your partner?

Developmental:

▶ How do you increase trust in yourself and others in your workplace?

Trust Zones

Frame It!

"Trust can be elusive; when it's present, it can be invisible. When it is absent, on the other hand, it is quite easy to see. If you choose to participate, this exercise will allow some of the ingredients of trust to come alive."

Objective

Navigate safely in pairs across the "Trust Zone" without hitting any objects of value

Guidelines

✓ Invite group to scatter things of value around the floor in the designated "Trust Zone" (e.g., wallets, phones, watches, bags, etc.)

✓ One partner must keep eyes closed while being led by a guide partner (whose eyes are open) through the "Trust Zone"

✓ Stay clear of any people or objects while navigating the Trust Zone

Trust

✓ *Round 1*: Navigate across in whatever way the pair decides

✓ *Round 2*: Navigate across without touching your partner at all

✓ *Round 3*: Navigate across without touching or talking to your partner

Tips

After *Round 1* ask: "What were specific behaviors that promoted trust?" Ask the group to apply these behaviors to the next round in order to build trust. This is an activity that requires the facilitator to maintain a keen eye toward risk management. Be ready to intervene if needed. Keep an eye on the objects of value that have been placed on the ground so nothing gets broken by mistake.

Trust

Debrief

Recreational:

▶ What strategies helped you build trust with your partner? Were there any times when trust began to falter? Which role was more challenging: "walker" or "guide"?

Educational:

▶ How did you manage times when trust faltered? How did you acknowledge your partner as trust was being built or rebuilt?

Developmental:

▶ When are you a "walker" at work? What do you do to support any people who are being your "guide"? When do you take on the role of a "guide" at work?

▶ How can you continue to build trust with your colleagues based on your experiences during this activity?

We! Connect
Card Activities

We! Connect Card™ activities are designed to transform conversation into action. Some activities are light and fun, while others introduce physical and emotional challenge. We intentionally created each activity write up to be brief to allow space for your own interpretation. Be creative in your facilitation! Mold each activity to best suit your group and your environment. Let the 60 questions within this deck spark powerful conversations aimed at developing relationships that last far beyond each of the following activities:

- ▶ Question Swap
- ▶ Conversation Roulette
- ▶ Me to We
- ▶ Ping
- ▶ Dialogue Data
- ▶ Freeze Action
- ▶ Mirror Neurons
- ▶ Poker Swap

About the Deck

We! Connect Cards

Create Conversations that Matter

60 qu
10+ a
Infinite con

www.weand.m

Each card has a question on one side and an action on the other. There are 20 purple cards, 20 green cards, and 20 blue cards in the deck. The three colors represents the type of question on that card as described below. This color code can be used as a tool to offer people more choice and autonomy in the types of conversations they will have.

We! Connect Cards

color code for type of questions

questions that encourage
SELF REFLECTION

questions that are
FUN AND LIGHT

questions that are
A BIT DEEPER

Actions shown on the back of each card can be used in a variety of ways to engage people depending the context, the group, and the goal of each activity. You can find video tutorials for these activities at:

www.weand.me/connect

No self survives a
conversation.

- David Whyte -

We make our
world significant
by the courage of
our questions and
the depth of our
answers.

— Carl Sagan —

Question
Swap

Watch a video tutorial at **www.weand.me/connect**

Frame It!

"You are the experts of your own experience. This activity is about sharing some of that knowledge."

Objective

Swap questions and answers to learn about the other people on your team

Guidelines

✓ After explaining the question color code system, have everyone choose a single card based on color

✓ Pair up with one other person to ask the question on your card, listen to your partner's response, and then answer the question on your partner's card

✓ Swap cards after each conversation and hold your card in the air to signal that you are looking for a new partner

✓ Continue connecting as long as the energy is high

Conversation
Roulette

Watch a video tutorial at www.wearod.me/connect

Frame It!

"We are going to get our brains free flowing a bit. Be prepared to think on your feet!"

Objective

Stretch your brain's capacity for on-the-spot thinking and sharing in preparation for a brainstorming session

Guidelines

√ Divide people into smaller groups of six or fewer

√ Give a pile of green cards to each small group

√ After explaining that green cards have questions that tend to be "fun and light," invite people to pick one card at a time, read the question, and offer their answer to the group as quickly as possible

√ Play until piles run out or the energy starts to slow

How would you like to be remembered?

Me to We

Watch a video tutorial at www.weand.me/connect

Frame It!

"Whether you are more introverted or extroverted, we could all do with a little time to think before we speak."

Objective

Share more authentic answers to personal questions to build a deeper understanding of who the people in the group really are

Guidelines

✓ Use **purple cards** for this activity (these questions are designed to encourage self-reflection)

✓ Invite each person to choose a purple card and then take 5 - 10 minutes alone in order to consider and then reflect upon their most genuine answer

✓ After the group comes back together, invite people to share their answers and reflections with the group

Ping

Watch a video tutorial at **www.weand.me/connect**

Frame It!

"What key questions does everyone ask on Mondays? 'How are you?' 'How was your weekend?' Routine questions often yield routine answers."

Objective

Select or create a question to replace the easy-to-ask questions that land us in "conversation ruts"

Guidelines

✓ Brainstorm and record a list of all the run-of-the-mill questions the groups finds themselves asking and answering (e.g., "How are you?")

✓ In small groups, sort an entire deck of We! Connect Cards into three piles: great questions, mediocre questions, and lousy questions

✓ As a group, choose a single question from the "great questions" pile to serve as a replacement for a routine questions (i.e., "ping")

Dialogue
Data

Watch a video tutorial at **www.weand.me/connect**

Frame It!

"Diversity in our comfort levels is what makes coming together so interesting!"

Objective

Choose cards/questions that match your comfort level to "take the temperature" of the group

Guidelines

✓ After explaining the question color code system, invite each person to pick up one to four cards of a color/question type of their choice

✓ Arrange the cards that are left by laying out cards of the same color one above the next to form a bar graph

✓ Ask the group to reflect on what this data says about the group (e.g., What does this say about the group's comfort level?)

✓ This activity can be added on to other activities like Question Swap or Poker Swap

We! Connect Cards™

work better, together

Freeze
Action

Watch a video tutorial at **www.weand.me/connect**

Frame It!

"Right now is your chance to create a movement and start 'the wave.'"

Objective

Get the entire group to freeze while walking and then as quickly as possible mimic the card action being modeled by the first group member who froze in place

Guidelines

✓ Start by having people walk quickly around a space in no particular formation

✓ Anyone can choose to freeze in place and do the action from the card back at anytime 15 - 20 seconds after each round begins

✓ As soon as you see somebody freeze in place and start doing an action, mimic that action as quickly as possible

✓ After a few rounds, have everyone take very sharp corners when turning to ramp up the energy

Mirror
Neurons

Watch a video tutorial at **www.weand.me/connect**

Frame It!

"There are neurons in our brain called mirror neurons which act as a biological way to imitate and connect with other people. This activity is all about activating our mirror neurons!"

Objective

Within a given time limit, kinesthetically (i.e., using actions and not words) find as many people with the same action as yours printed on their card

Guidelines

✓ Each person can pick a card with an action of their choice

✓ Silently form a pair with someone else in the group, make eye contact, and simultaneously do the action described on each of your cards

✓ If you discover that you and your partner have the same action, celebrate with a high five, swap cards, and continue trying to find as many other people in the group as possible who share your action

✓ If you discover that you and your partner have a different action, quickly swap cards with each other, give them a fist bump, and move on to finding others who might share your new action

Tips

This activity can be an energizer or a way to calmly wind down at the end of a day, depending on how you frame it.

We! Connect Cards™

Poker
Swap

Watch a video tutorial at www.weand.me/connect

Frame It!

"Great questions can create great conversations. And conversations are the source of connection."

Objective

Design a great conversation to get to know one another better by trading cards to create an ideal question set

Guidelines

✓ Each person chooses three cards from the deck at random

✓ Five minutes is given during which people may go question shopping from other peoples' cards

✓ People may trade multiple cards, but may only trade a maximum of one card with any other participant

✓ After five minutes, invite people to "pair up with someone who they would like to get to know better" for 10 - 15 minutes, using their combined six questions to fuel their conversation

Sample Program Designs

Now it is time to put it all together. The following pages contain sequences we designed to help you begin to create a great experiential program for your group. These sequences are simply frameworks for you to build upon and customize for your group.

Networking Sequences

These two networking sequences will provide 30 minutes to 1 hour of activities to build community and encourage individuals to build relationships. They can be facilitated with any size group.

Networking Sequence #1

▶ Ubuntu Fast Find
▶ Who?
▶ Handshakes
▶ Ubuntu Olympics
▶ Incorporations

Networking Sequence #2

▶ Who?
▶ We! Connect Cards - Question Swap
▶ We! Connect Cards - Dialogue Data
▶ We! Connect Cards - Conversation Roulette
▶ We! Connect Cards - Ping

Half-Day Sequences

We design our programs around the specific needs of our clients. The sample program flows listed below offer examples of how you might choose to sequence some of the activities in this guide. A half day is usually considered to be 3 - 4 hours of programmed time. Often, we facilitate these programs for intact teams of 8 - 12 participants each. The sequences that follow will help groups work on:

- ✓ Getting to know each other
- ✓ Sharpening communication skills
- ✓ Further developing cooperation skills
- ✓ Building trust
- ✓ Exploring group problem solving

Half-Day Sequence #1

- ▶ Who?
- ▶ Ubuntu Fast Find
- ▶ Handshakes
- ▶ Group Juggle
- ▶ Paper Tower
- ▶ Paired Compass Walk
- ▶ Keypunch
- ▶ Trust Zone
- ▶ Zin Monument

Half-Day Sequence #2

- ▶ What's in a Name?
- ▶ We! Connect Cards - Question Swap
- ▶ We! Connect Cards - Me to We
- ▶ We! Connect Cards - Mirror Neurons
- ▶ We! Discover Cards - Travel the World
- ▶ Keypunch
- ▶ Zin Monument
- ▶ Trust Zones

Resource List

Unsurprisingly, there are a lot of excellent resources available that don't quite fit into our "pocket guide." Many of these resources are provided by our friends, partners, and colleagues in the field of experiential training and development. Here is your one stop shop for a plethora of great resources to help you create powerful human connections.

Materials

▶ We! Connect Cards™ (**www.weand.me/store**)
▶ We! Discover Cards™ (**www.weand.me/store**)
▶ Body Part Debrief (www.training-wheels.com)
▶ Ubuntu Cards (www.high5adventure.org)

Websites

▶ Video tutorials for We! Connect Cards™
   (**www.weand.me/connect**)
▶ playmeo: World's largest database of experiential activities (**www.weand.me/playmeo**)

Books

▶ *The Hundredth Monkey* (2012) by Nate Folan

▶ *Serious Fun* (2014) by Mark Collard

▶ *The Processing Pinnacle* (2006) by Steven Simpson, Dan Miller, and Buzz Bocher

▶ *Tips and Tools: The Art of Experiential Group Facilitation* (2008) by Jennifer Stanchfield

▶ *The Best Advice So Far* (2014) by Erik Tyler

Science

The ideas within this book stand on the shoulders of giants. Below is a list of academic and practitioner resources from which we gleaned our some of our inspiration. Research shows the value of human connection and concrete experience with regard to the learning process. The teams of people referenced below have dedicated their lives to uncovering the details and the data to support that claim.

Albanese, R. (1994). Team-building process: key to better project results.Journal of Management in Engineering, 10(6), 36-44.

Baker, A. C., Jensen, P. J., & Kolb, D. A. (2005). Conversation as experiential learning. Management learning, 36(4), 411-427.

Bransford, J., Stevens, R., Schwartz, D., Meltzoff, A. N., Pea, R., Roschelle, J., Vye, N., Kuhl, P. K., Bell, P., Barron,B., Reeves, B., & Sabelli, N. (2006). Learning theories and education: Toward a decade of synergy. Handbook of educational psychology. Mahwah, NJ: Erlbaum.

Carmeli, A., Brueller, D., & Dutton, J. E. (2009). Learning behaviours in the workplace: The role of high-quality interpersonal relationships and psychological safety. Systems Research and Behavioral Science.

Chlup, D. T., & Collins, T. E. (2010). Breaking the Ice: Using Icebreakers and Re-Energizers with Adult Learners. Adult Learning, 21, 34-39.

Collard, M. (2005). No props: Great games with no equipment.

Cressey, P., Exton, R., & Totterdill, P. (2013). Workplace social dialogue as a form of "productive reflection." International Journal of Action, 9(2), 209–245.

Crookall, D. (2010). Serious games, debriefing, and simulation/gaming as a discipline. Simulation & Gaming, 41(6), 898-920.

Damasio, A. (2005). Human behavior: Brain trust. Nature, 435(June), 571–572.

Garrick, J. (1998). Informal learning in corporate workplaces. Human Resource Development Quarterly, 9(2), 129–144.

Kapp, E. (2009). Improving student teamwork in a collaborative project-based course. College Teaching, 57(3), 139-143.

Kayes, A. B., Kayes, D. C., & Kolb, D. A. (2005). Experiential learning in teams. Simulation & Gaming, 36(3), 330-354.

Kolb, D.A. (1984). Experiential learning: experience as the source of learning and development

McLeod, S. (2010). Zone of proximal development. Retrieved May, 19, 2013.

Iacoboni, M. (2009). Imitation, empathy, and mirror neurons. Annual review of psychology, 60, 653-670.

Illeris, K. (2007). What Do We Actually Mean by Experiential Learning? Human Resource Development Review, 6(1), 84–95.

Martin, A. J., & Dowson, M. (2009). Interpersonal relationships, motivation, engagement, and achievement: Yields for theory, current issues, and educational practice. Review of Educational Research, 79(1), 327-365.

Nelson, H. G., & Stolterman, E. (2003). The design way: Intentional change in an unpredictable world: Foundations and fundamentals of design competence. Educational Technology.

Piaget, J. (1971). The theory of stages in cognitive development.

Raz, A. E., & Fadlon, J. (2006). Managerial culture, workplace culture and situated curricula in organizational learning. Organization Studies.

Richardson, P., & Denton, D. K. (2005). How to create a high-performance team. Human Resource Development Quarterly, 16(3), 417–423.

Rogoff, B. (1990). Apprenticeship in thinking: Cognitive development in social context. Oxford University Press.

Sorensen, B. M., & Spoelstra, S. (2011). Play at work: continuation, intervention and usurpation. Organization, 19(1), 81–97.

Sense, A. J. (2005). Facilitating conversational learning in a project team practice. Journal of Workplace Learning, 17(3), 178-193.

Tamir, D. I., & Mitchell, J. P. (2012). Disclosing information about the self is intrinsically rewarding. Proceedings of the National Academy of Sciences,109(21), 8038-8043.

Thiagarajan, S. (1992). Using games for debriefing. Simulation & gaming, 23(2), 161-173.

Thiagarajan, S. (1991). Garbage A Card Game that Simulates the Trade-Off between Competition and Concern. Simulation & Gaming, 22(1), 112-115.

Wenger, E. C., & Snyder, W. M. (2000). Communities of practice: The organizational frontier. Harvard business review, 78(1), 139-146.

Williams, S. D., Graham, T. S., & Baker, B. (2003). Evaluating outdoor experiential training for leadership and team building. Journal of Management Development, 22(1), 45-59.

Rod Lee

Rod Lee is SVP of Client
Engagement for upstage,
based in the United States. He
delivers programs worldwide utilizing experiential,
classroom, and virtual delivery modes. Over the past
two decades, he has designed and facilitated single-
and multi-day, customized learning programs on
topics including Team and Leadership Development,
Cross Cultural Competence, Global Team Leadership,
Leading Remote Teams, Motivation, Communication,
and Presentation Skills.

Rod's key clients:

- ▶ AccuWeather
- ▶ Baker Tilly
- ▶ BP
- ▶ Dell Boomi
- ▶ General Mills
- ▶ Oracle
- ▶ PepsiCo
- ▶ NetSuite
- ▶ Penn State University
- ▶ SAS
- ▶ SiriusDecisions
- ▶ University of New Hampshire

 www.upstage-engages.com

 rod@upstagecommunications.com

 @RoderickMLee

Chad Littlefield

Chad Littlefield, M.Ed., is the co-founder and CEO of We!™

Leaders call Chad when a lack of trust gets in the way of results. Chad is a speaker and professional facilitator. He designs fun, challenging, and engaging experiences and tools that break down communication barriers. He has spoken at TEDx and is also the creator of *We! Connect Cards*™, which are now being used to **create conversations that matter** in over 50 countries around the world and on 6 of the 7 continents.

Chad lives in Asheville, NC with his wonderful wife, Kate. They both enjoy traveling often for business and adventure.